LEATHERCRAFT

- MATERIALS AND TOOLS, CONSTRUCTION METHODS, GENERAL WORKING HINTS AND FORMS OF DECORATION -

BY

P. WYLIE DAVIDSON

Copyright © 2011 Read Books Ltd.
This book is copyright and may not be
reproduced or copied in any way without
the express permission of the publisher in writing

British Library Cataloguing-in-Publication Data
A catalogue record for this book is available from
the British Library

LEATHERCRAFT

P. WYLIE DAVIDSON

LEATHERWORK as a craft offers an unlimited and increasing field of interest. To the home-worker it has a definite appeal. Commercially it offers unrivalled possibilities to the professional craftsman. As a discipline and training for hand and eye it is invaluable in the schoolroom, while for the retired business man or woman it provides a pleasant pastime. The art of the leather-worker is a craft with a history, and although its origin is lost in the age of romance, it still retains a certain spirit of the past. Even in this machine age, with its multiple production, a piece of genuine hand-tooled leather is something to treasure. The leather itself is a beautiful and desirable medium to handle, with endless possibilities for use and ornament. Its surface responds readily to the impression of the tool, and in the hands of a keen worker definite progress is assured. In the design and execution of leatherwork, aim exclusively at the free and correct use of the material, which is the secret of all true craftsmanship. Tool application alone is too often a mere surface ornamentation of elaborate markings. The more desirable result is obtainable only when the tool is used during the actual production of the work.

THONGING, LACING AND PLAITING. These are the perfect and ideal decorations and suggest the natural treatment for leatherwork. Leather thongs of varied colour, length and thickness are themselves an inspiration to new and fresh ideas in working the material. They stimulate and develop the creative faculty of the worker and save him from becoming a mere copyist. This happy co-operation of hand and brain is the ideal of all craftsmanship. Undeniably, the craft is one which calls forth all our skill and inventive genius, whether in the evolution of new designs and original treatment or in the choice of tools and materials.

THE VARIOUS SKINS AND THEIR USES. In purchasing leather for any purpose, always insist on the best quality. Good work is impossible on inferior material. Purchase the leather of the size and shape required, unless there is an immediate prospect of using the entire skin. As the majority of manufacturers supply leather for all kinds of purposes, no difficulty will be experienced in suiting one's requirements. Certain parts of a hide are preferable ; the leather cut from the back will furnish the most desirable surface. Other parts of the hide will be excellent for smaller articles, such as gussets and interiors, or sides for a box. Keep the leather, when not in use, perfectly flat, as it is most irritating to work if a curl is developed. The following list of leathers, with brief notes on their special uses, will prove helpful to the worker.

THE VARIOUS SKINS. There are Calfskin, Persians, Chamois, Cowhide, Goatskin, Patent and Fancy Leathers, Sheepskin or Basil, Pigskin, Skiver, and Doeskin.

CALFSKIN is the ideal surface for a tooled and modelled decoration. On a soft and well-chosen skin, previously prepared by a thorough immersion in water, the slightest impress of the tool will result in pleasing outlines of light and shade. It is a most adaptable medium and may be employed for practically every variety of work. It will respond beautifully to the cuts of the incising knife or chisel. It also takes stains freely and true to colour. Colour schemes applied with the brush or the spray will prove equally effective on its surface. Even simple tool impressions on the damp leather will result in ideal harmonies of russet brown.

COWHIDE is naturally of a more robust texture. Its weight makes it suitable for strong and enduring work. It may be obtained with an undressed or polished surface. It may also be had for special bags, with the natural hair of the animal adhering to the skin.

SHEEPSKIN OR BASIL is not a skin to recommend for special work as it is very cheap and its quality varies greatly. Good results may be obtained from hammering applied, as in repoussé, to its surface. It may be recommended for beginners.

SKIVER (split sheepskin) is extremely serviceable for linings. Its light and pliable nature makes it excellent for interiors and fittings, and in combination with light strawboard it is used as a backing for many varieties of inside fittings. It will also take colour freely when applied with the spray, but is not too suitable for work with the brush, where it is liable to give irregular washes. The skins are not costly and are sold entire.

PERSIANS (velvet and plain) may be obtained in a large variety of colourings. They are well adapted for articles of daily wear such as golf jackets, hats, slippers, cushions and articles of a like nature. In the schoolroom they will be found useful in the production of articles which for their decorative effect depend mainly on plain surfaces with perfectly thonged borders. Such work affords excellent practice to the hand and eye of a young student.

GOATSKIN is the skin from which the finest morocco leather is derived. Genuine morocco is a most beautiful material in texture and pliability, and for covering books, caskets and all leatherwork demanding quality and beauty it is invaluable. Many passable imitations can be had, and carefully treated, they serve quite well for certain types of work.

PIGSKIN is naturally of a strong durable and tough nature, and slightly oily texture. For shopping bags, book-bindings and heavy thongings it will be found most suitable.

LEATHERCRAFT

DOESKIN has a fine silky texture and may be obtained in numerous shades. It is much in favour with costumiers; also in the production of small sundries embracing buttons, belts, footwear and gloves.

CHAMOIS or wash leather is delightfully pliable and soft in texture. It is useful where soft machine-stitched linings are required for bags, gloves and similar articles of leatherware.

ENAMELLED OR PATENT LEATHER is extremely useful decoratively. It may be obtained in all colours and is especially appropriate where a rich bright spot of strong colour is required. Its firm, glazed surface stands fairly hard wear and may be washed freely. It looks at its best when introduced in pleasing shapes and in small sections in boxes, belts, mocassins and other small articles. It is inexpensive and may be purchased in the multiple stores in the form of cheap belts.

THE NECESSARY TOOLS

THE tools required for leathercraft are few and inexpensive. Quite good and pleasing results are possible with an extremely limited outfit. Thus with a single modeller, small hammer or mallet, footrule and thonging punch one may produce passable work.

AGATE POINT OR STYLUS. This tool is used in transferring the design to the leather. (Substitute: knitting needle or hard pencil.)

MODELLING TOOL. An indispensable tool for all modelled and embossed patterns. Procure one with a blunt and sharp terminal to act as a tracer; an additional tool with curved section, blunt at one end and sharp at the other, will also be helpful.

DRESDEN TOOL. A necessary requisite for setting and laying a background; it is also useful as a modeller.

BULL TOOL. This tool is utilised for embossing from the obverse side of the skin. Procure one with a small and one with a large bullet head.

REPOUSSÉ HAMMER OR LIGHT MALLET. The steel hammer is preferable as it may be put to a greater variety of uses. Avoid too heavy a tool.

SHOEMAKER'S KNIFE. A cheap and indispensable requisite. Excellent for cutting the leather into any desired size or shape. It will also pare the edges where lapping over of the material is required.

INCISING KNIFE. This tool serves to outline the design where cut leather decoration is desired. It will also cut stencils, etc. (Substitute: an ordinary penknife, well sharpened.)

REVOLVING PUNCH PLIERS. A necessary tool with its graded punches for perforating the holes to receive the thongs. With such a tool, properly used, a row of thonging will become a thing of beauty.

THONGING PUNCH. A single tool required for piercing holes in parts of the work which are inaccessible to the punch pliers. It is chiefly used for leather edgings. This punch in two sizes would be found most convenient.

SLITTING PUNCH. For horizontal slit holes, which in certain types of work are more suitable as they take a tighter grip on the thongs without leaving a space at the thonging.

ORDINARY SCISSORS. An essential part of the leatherworker's equipment.

LEAD BLOCK. A block of scrap lead moulded to a circular or square shape, 1 inch thick and 3 inches in diameter. It is a most useful implement. On its surface all manner of holes may be punched without any chance of spoiling the face of the tool.

FOOTRULE—BRASS OR WOOD. Avoid steel: it soils leather.

STEEL DIVIDERS. For setting out the thonging, and arranging all manner of spacing.

SET SQUARE. Necessary for setting out patterns.

WOODCARVER'S CHISELS. Several of the larger and smaller straight and half-chisels are especially adapted for the direct piercing of stencilled leather.

SHEET OF PLATE-GLASS OR A LARGE TILE. One of these will be required when modelling leather to ensure the correct working conditions. Wood or cardboard should not be used as they absorb the water from the leather.

DRAWING PINS AND PAPER. Necessary requisites. The paper should be thin but strong to ensure a ready response from the tracing point in transferring the design to the leather. White foolscap (plain) is quite suitable.

SPONGE. Sponging is necessary to preserve the dampness of the leather when one is modelling.

REPOUSSÉ PUNCHES. Two repoussé punches (outliners) will be found useful. They may both be straight, with one sharp in section and the other blunt.

REPOUSSÉ PUNCH. One square backgrounder will serve for setting the background of the work.

With the above assortment of tools, anyone who has the slightest aptitude for drawing may take up leathercraft with every prospect of success. As the worker progresses, the following additional list of tools and material will be helpful.

SET OF SADDLER'S PUNCHES. Extremely helpful in piercing holes of graded size; ovals and other varied shapes may also be obtained, and with their use delightful stencilled borders and patterns may be devised.

LEATHERCRAFT

LACING TOOL. With three cutting phases. Useful where straight, direct incisions are required.

SPUR WHEEL. On the run will provide a succession of stitching holes, or by missing one incision the alternate mark will serve for thonging.

MODELLING WHEEL. Extremely useful for tracing long, continuous lines, it is easily and quickly applied.

PINKING IRONS. Applied on edges to give a decorative and effective finish on certain types of work.

SCREW CREASER. They are also used for edgings where indented lines are required on margins. They are made in single and double lines, which are interchangeable.

PRESS STUD COMBINATION. Punches and die. They are made of brass, simple and inexpensive, and are required for locking the press studs on leatherware.

LIGHT RIVETTING HAMMER. With round and oblong face. When rivets are used it is required to fix the rivet heads.

FANCY PUNCHES (steel or brass). Will be found useful on small articles demanding a decoration of all-over pattern or running borders.

BOOKBINDER'S STAMPS. These are made of brass and are applied in blind tooling; also in the use of gold and silver leaf.

SMALL SPRAY. Necessary for the application of the stains, where a stippled or uniform surface is desired.

SEWING AWL (the Gem). Simple and extremely serviceable for hand-sewn work.

FRET-SAW AND BLADES. Necessary where small metal fittings are introduced.

BENCH VICE (strong). Indispensable where advanced work has to be considered.

GOLD, SILVER AND BRONZE LEAF. This may be bought in convenient book form (free fixed).

BONE FOLDER. An extremely useful implement for pressing and assembling parts where paste or a similar fixitive is in use.

COLOUR STAINS. These may be obtained in all colours and in convenient forms for application. They may be obtained in powder or liquid form. The powder stain is dissolved in methylated spirits before application. Coloured inks are useful for fine details of rich tone; they will also give a pen line which at times is very effective. Water colours can also be utilised but they must be wax polished or they are liable to fade.

FILES (half-round). Several are necessary where hinges, lettering or metal fittings are applied.

PLIERS (round and flat). Will prove extremely helpful on various occasions.

SMALL DRILL STOCK. With drills may be required in the fixing of metal sundries on leatherware.

LEATHERCRAFT

Various sundries, including the following, can all be utilised. Platinum point for leather tinting, brass scratch brush, box of small brass clips, eyelet pliers, leather polishing cream, pastes and fixitives, gold size, also several brushes.

Constructional Methods

CONSTRUCTIONAL methods in leatherware are a vitally important part of the craft. Before any article in leather is actually begun it should be drafted out, full size, on cartridge paper. If it is a bag, add on the necessary allowance for depth at bottom and sides in the correct shapes, and sketch in the flap and position of fastenings. Cut out and fold the whole and adjust until its proportions give perfect satisfaction. The bag may be entirely plain, but its design will prove satisfying with good proportion, pleasing outline and perfect thonging. In the construction of articles in leather, give utility the first and rightful place, allowing any decoration to be a secondary consideration. Press studs and all types of fasteners are important and necessary articles in constructional work. They must be placed in their correct position, and always with a clear space between them and the thonging. Many a passable piece of work is ruined by having press studs placed in a bad position. When fixing in a stud secure the button, or face, of the stud first. Place it exactly in the centre of the bag front and apply sufficient pressure to mark its position. Over a surface of wood or lead punch a hole large enough to admit the large washer. *Do not* have the hole too large or the stud will become loose. Now reverse the flap of the bag and rest it on the small brass die supplied with the stud set. Insert the *large punch* into the washer and give it a solid blow, *revolving* the punch as you do so. Press the *large stud*, which is now in position on the flap, against the front and centre of the bag. The impression obtained will give the exact position of the small *socket or head*. Apply the small punch to suit the *washer*, and then insert the socket from the inside of the bag—a blow from the tabular punch will effectively lock the washer. The snap may now be tested. If too easy-fitting, give the small socket a gentle tap with a light hammer to spread it slightly. If too tight a delicate squeeze with small pliers around its circumference will ease it slightly.

INTERIOR FITTINGS. Interior fittings in skiver or suède should all be sketched out on thin paper before cutting the skin. They may be grouped and stitched together by machine in detail as desired, and finally thonged into the bag itself.

LININGS. These may be secured with any well-tested fixitive.

GUSSETS. Gussets may be applied as a continuous band of leather, as in an oblong or square shopping bag. They may also be cut to a U shape where side insertions are desired. A side gusset, after lining, may be thoroughly softened with water, doubled over in the centre, and then placed on a surface of glass with a heavy weight over it. This will provide spring or hinge so necessary in a bag.

Gussets Unusual or Irregular in Shape. These may be fashioned by softening the leather thoroughly with water, and then modelling and binding them over a wire to any section. When the correct form is attained place a weight over them until completely dry. The U-shaped gusset will fit the bag better if a small slit is introduced at the bottom of the gusset. Carefully count and arrange the thonging holes on the gusset to ensure perfect fitting.

Bag Handles. Bag handles of plaited thongs, single or in groups, should always have the ends of the thongs hidden, either inside the bag or between the outer surface and the lining.

Thong Ends. These should all be laced inside and under the thonging; a touch of durofix or seccotine may be applied to render them secure.

Lightning Fasteners—How to Fix Them. Fold the tape on each side of the fastener and stitch securely to the leather with linen thread, allowing a clear space of at least $\frac{3}{16}$ of an inch between the metal and the edge of the article, thus affording perfect action for the fastener. Keep the fastener closed when it is being attached. If sewn in when open it is liable to have a faulty action. Finish by fastening the lower end of the fastener securely.

In constructional work in leather the various manufacturers make a point of providing all possible requisites, so no difficulty should be experienced by the aspiring worker in becoming fairly proficient in this beautiful " old-time " craft.

Educational Notes and Pointers on Leathercraft

Thonged edges on pocket-books, purses, pochettes and similar small articles are much improved by spreading the thonging to a uniform flat surface with a wooden mallet on a clean table.

Thonging Holes on gussets and semi-circular corners are better when kept slightly closer than on straight edges, to ensure more compact fitting.

Gold Thonging. When this is applied along an edge which is to be overcast with another thong, it is advisable to " tack " the end of the gold thong with a fixitive. This method will secure it in position and allow greater liberty in the application of the other thong.

Gold, Silver and Copper Bronze. These details in the form of circles may be stamped with the circular thonging punches, and equivalent holes in a decoration pierced to contain them. A final fixing with durofix or seccotine will be required.

BAG HANDLES. As a general rule in constructional work, bag handles should be inserted between the lining and the bag; also securely fixed to the bag itself by the use of small half thongs skilfully and decoratively applied.

LEATHER CUT TO CIRCLES. When leather is cut to circles, squares and similar shapes provide interesting units of decoration They may be assembled in sections of different colour and superimposed on each other. Fix them finally from the centre with "cloutage" nails or a gold thong.

"CLOUTAGE" AND ALL NAILS. These are more easily applied to wood, etc., if they are pushed into a piece of hard soap before their insertion.

SHRINKAGE. In large areas of leather always make a slight allowance for shrinkage.

PENCIL AND CARBON PAPER. These must be carefully applied as they are liable to soil the delicate skin; use them only on the obverse when embossing.

LEATHER. Leather of reasonable weight, and thoroughly dry, may be cut and carved to any desired section and thickness.

GOLD AND SILVER THONGS. Gold and silver thongs may be effectively plaited together to give pleasing variety to the pattern.

TOOLED LINES IN LEATHER. These look best when applied in groups, also with one line narrow and the other broad.

INTERLACING THONGS. Interlacing thongs to fit a flat decoration of Celtic style must have the small, curved angles cut direct from the skin to the curve required. These units of leather are then slipped in to run in harmony with the other lines.

THONGS. Good effects are obtained by tooling a narrow deep line in the centre of the thong, after the completion of the lacing.

PRESS STUDS. Press studs may with excellent results be introduced as part of the design. For example, the stem of a modelled flower, the spiral of a scroll line, may be arranged to radiate from the press stud. Press studs may be stripped of the cellular cover and have gold, silver or enamel substituted to suit different articles and colour schemes.

GOLD LEAF. Apply fixed gold in book form; it will be easier to transfer to the leather.

DIES. Cut with a chisel to any size, depth or outline on a block of wood, will provide a convenient means of embossing damp leather without disturbing the level of the surrounding surface.

BACKGROUNDS ON LEATHER. When using the background punch hold it perfectly perpendicular to ensure a solid and flat impression.

INLAID LEATHER. Cut the stencil on the leather and the units for insertion all from the same weight of skin, to ensure a uniform and perfectly flat surface when the work is completed.

WATER COLOURS. Added to leather these are liable to be

fugitive; they will require a thin film of clear varnish as a protective medium.

COLOURED INKS. These provide an ideal medium for true, rich and permanent colour; they may also be applied in hair line, dots and all fine detail.

OIL COLOURS. Oil colours may be applied to leather, but they must be thinned down to ensure their transparency.

GOLD TOOLING. To ensure complete success with the application of gold, in any form, to a surface of leather, repeated washings with paste water are necessary to overcome the porous nature of the leather. The final addition of the " glaire," carefully applied, will provide a perfect result.

BLIND TOOLING. This may be carried out on dry or wet leather; better and more permanent impressions are obtained on the damp surface. If the brass stamps are slightly warm a pleasing rich brown tone will result.

THE BOOKING STAMPS. In the application of the stamps to the leather always test the degree of heat by inserting them in a wet pad of cotton wool. When the " hiss " is off the tool, polish the stamp on a scrap of leather and apply it to the surface to be decorated.

METAL STAMPS. Metal stamps or punch should not be heated but applied cold with the hammer blow.

SETTING OF BACKGROUNDS. In laying a background on any decoration note carefully that the entire area of leather next the outline must be perfectly treated, otherwise the design will lack the smart, clean effect necessary in cut or modelled leather.

BLIND TOOLING. An intricate pattern in blind tooling preparatory to the use of gold may be impressed through a surface of thin paper with the design upon its surface.

MODELLED LEATHER: METHODS

MODELLED leather is probably the most popular of all the decorative forms, although in the majority of cases its artistic value and standard of craftsmanship does not compare with good sound thonging. Still it is the vogue of the moment and offers a decided appeal to all workers in the craft. It is admirably suited for the decoration of bags, blotters, music satchels and panels. It is also utilised on chairbacks, mural panels, and may be seen on some of the modern furniture where a bold and durable treatment is necessary.

MODELLING: CHOICE OF THE DESIGN. A modelled decoration on leather may be applied in many different ways in accordance with the nature of the object and scale of the work. Panels of a small area, suitable for pochettes, pocket-books or book-covers, will naturally demand quiet but interesting details principally in bas-relief. To obtain this effect the necessary amount of pressure must be carefully judged in carrying out the various details of a well-considered scheme of varied outline and section. The intro-

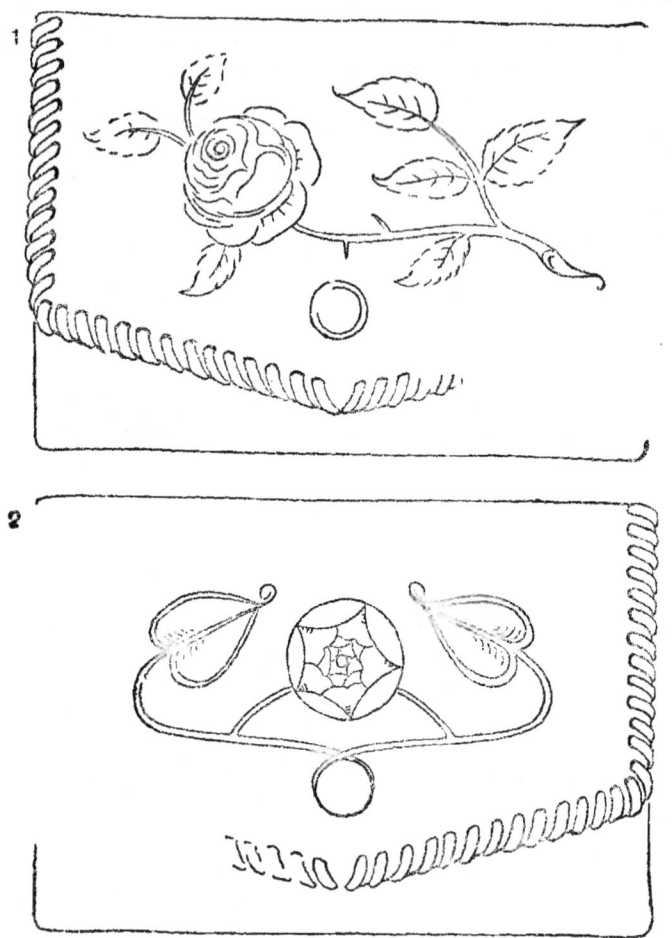

Design in modelling bas-relief. 1. Realistic treatment. 2. Conventional treatment.

duction of broad, soft hollows throughout the design, and the contrast of the thick and thin line on the velvety surface of the calfskin are always pleasing. This is termed flat modelling. It is the simplest and most elementary form of leather decoration, a treatment which will be found most suitable for the beginner. Larger objects will require a design of a stronger and more definite character. In designing for leatherware, as a decorative production,

3. Simple line tooled borders.

avoid any attempt to copy nature in realistic forms. Figures, animals, birds, fish, flowers, fruit and leaves provide ideal motifs for decoration as applied to leather, but their use and treatment, to be a success, must be subjected entirely to the possibilities of the tools and the material.

In choosing a design for leatherwork, irrespective of the type of leather, a clear appreciation of the construction and utility of the article will prove extremely helpful. Never overload a surface with useless and uninteresting ornament. Keep the arrangement of line and form as simple as possible. Always preserve a clear surface between the design and the thonging, and keep it well away from a press stud and other fastener.

RELATIONSHIP OF THE DECORATION TO THE THONGING. Again, remember that neat and uniform thonging is a complete decoration in itself. Therefore preserve it. Bold running borders of repeating pattern parallel with the outlines of the object also prove extremely satisfying on leatherwork, while a modelled design is greatly enhanced by a narrow laced border enclosing the modelled surface. Borders of this type lend themselves to a great variety of treatment.

APPLYING THE DESIGN TO THE LEATHER. With the design carefully drawn and ready for transferring, place the surface of leather for modelling on a smooth table or drawing-board. If the sheet-glass or tile suggested in the list of tools is available use it. Glass is particularly suitable since it does not absorb water. Only when the leather is *perfectly dry* must the design be transferred to it, for, though leather will respond more easily to pressure when damp, its surface is far too liable to acquire a dirty and soiled appearance. If the surface to be modelled is large, such as a panel, blotter or large bag, it may be pinned to a wooden board with drawing pins placed where they will not in any way injure the leather surface. Another simple method of securing the design while transferring it, is to weight the drawing down sufficiently to secure it in position, adjusting the weight as the work proceeds.

When the design has been carefully impressed with the stylus examine the result and deepen any part which may have been overlooked. Then place the leather under a running tap until both sides of the skin are thoroughly soaked, making sure that the whole surface has been covered. This precaution is

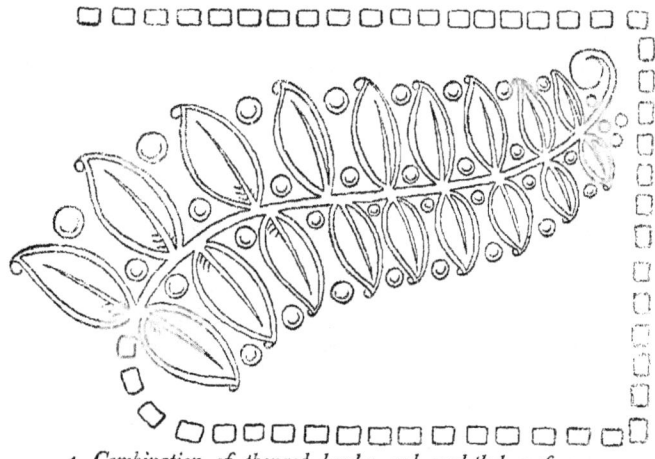

4. *Combination of thonged border and modelled surfaces.*

absolutely necessary, otherwise there will be a watermark. But after the first immersion the leather may be wetted in parts as desired with a small clean sponge without a blemish resulting. If a specially large surface has to be tooled, it is advisable to allow it to remain under water for several hours beforehand, then place it on a clean table to dry a little before using the modeller. This brings the leather to perfect condition for working. Now place two or three sheets of soft newspaper on the glass, and over that lay the leather with the design attached to it. The newspaper provides the pressure of the modelling tool with the ideal yielding resistance necessary to form the design into soft, modelled surfaces.

TOOLING AND EMBOSSING. Now with the blunt outliner (straight end) incise firmly over the entire outline, keeping the tool in a fairly flat position all the time.

APPLICATION OF THE BLUNT OUTLINER. When you are using

this tool avoid a monotonous, uniform line. Vary the tool-pressure at several points and you will give an agreeable variety of light and shade to the work. Again, in a modelled surface, if you " lose and follow " the outline occasionally, the result is extremely pleasing to the eye and gives a suggestion of the pattern melting into the leather. It also provides an opportunity for the craftsman to express a certain individuality of tooling. All the embossed parts will be tooled from the obverse side, using the ball-faced modeller.

APPLICATION OF THE BALL-FACED MODELLER. A good method of obtaining the desired relief without affecting the level of the surrounding of leather is to press the parts in section over a prepared square of wood with incised hollows on its surface. It will

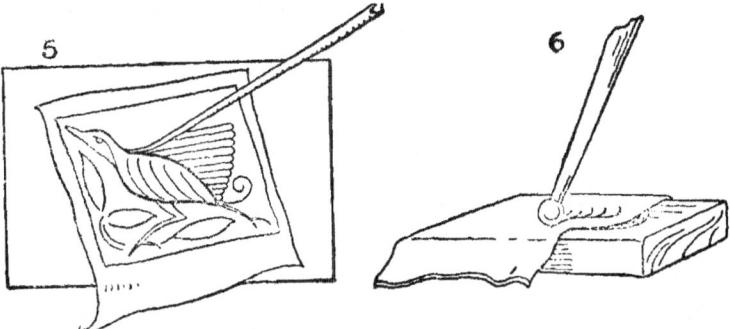

5. Illustrates use of blunt outliner showing the padding of newspaper between the leather and the glass. 6. Illustrates the use of the ball-faced modeller over a prepared block of wood.

be found very convenient to have one of these at hand. Take a block of wood with one surface about 5 inches square, and on it make shallow cavities in such shapes as circles, ovals and leaf-forms. Another method of treating embossed sections from the obverse side of the leather is to rest the skin on a flat pad of plastic wax and, with the ball-shaped modeller, press the leather forward. When completed reverse the work and tool the various details from the front. Bold surfaces of light and shade may be emphasised in parts of the outline as a fitting contrast to the more delicate sections of the work. Modelling clay may also be used as a surface for embossing, but it will require a sheet of waterproof paper on its face to safeguard the leather from soiling. The background of the design may be set down with the bent modeller while the damp leather is resting on the plate-glass surface, and all the time you are working on it retain the pad of paper between the glass and the leather. On the completion of the tooling, modelling and laying of the ground, fill in the concave sections on the obverse side with

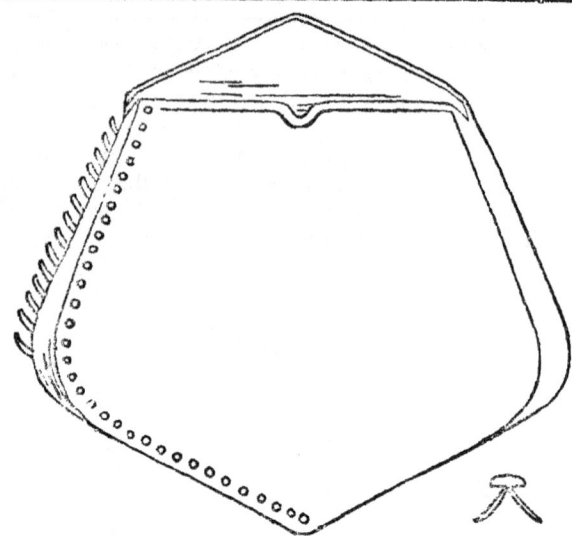

7. Bag clipped together and holed ready for thonging.

cotton wool and seccotine. A layer of mull as used by the bookbinder will bind all the parts together and final lining with leather will cover this binding neatly.

MURAL PANEL : DECORATION IN LEATHER EMBRACING TOOLING AND MODELLING, STAINING, THONGING AND INLAYING. When the modelling is completed the entire surface should be polished to preserve it from dust and general wear. Apply the polish on a small pad of cotton wool with a smart circular action until the " blush " of the skin appears, and finish with a chamois leather. Remember that thongs should be polished on the entire length and before thonging up the work.

HAMMERED LEATHERWORK, REPOUSSÉ AND BLIND TOOLING

A DECORATION in hammered leather naturally suggests the use of the hammer and the punch, a form of working comparable to repoussé in metalwork. The necessary tools include a hammer or mallet, with one or two blunt outliners, and a square backgrounder. The tracers, or outliners, will incise the pattern to a moderate depth, and the backgrounder will be employed to set down the surrounding surface of leather.

Repoussé on leather is well adapted for large and bold designs. Rest the leather on a flat board of soft wood. A few double sheets of newspaper placed between the leather and the board will give the correct resistance to the tool. In the case of the outliner avoid too great regularity ; vary the line in parts to intensify the shadows on the damp leather. Equally satisfactory results are obtained by the use of the outliners alone with a simple pattern of tooled lines.

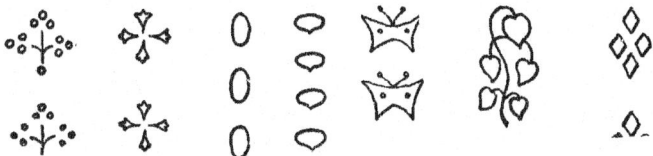

8. Patterns obtained by blind tooling and application of colour in ink and wax.

They may be utilised as borders of straight, curved, or interlacing lines. Some of the incisions may be broad and others of hair-line width as a contrast. On note-cases, pochettes and pocket-books this treatment is extremely effective.

HAMMERED LEATHERWORK EXAMPLE. Blind tooling is also a recognised form of hammered leather. It is produced mainly by the application of steel punches of varying pattern and size. This treatment may be executed on dry leather, and as a form of tooling it has much to commend it. The beginner with a limited range of tools and the exercise of a little thought can easily design patterns with the use of the tools as units. The clean-cut impression of the punch on the leather, easily obtained from the hammer blow, is always effective, and never more so than on the natural leather. It also conveys a happy suggestion of handwork by the slight irregularity which contrasts with the mechanical uniformity of machine production. Apply the steel punches only when cold. The incisions of the blind tooling may have a colour scheme applied to the depressions with a small brush. If the stamps are fine in detail, coloured inks applied with the pen will be found most suitable. A final rub with leather polish will provide the necessary finish to the entire work.

Unique results are also obtainable by the use of coloured wax applied to the sections of blind tooling. Dissolve the wax in methylated spirit to a convenient liquid form, applying it thinly to the stampings with a small brush or pen. When allowed to set and afterwards polished, quite an unusual decoration will be attained. This style is well adapted to all-over patterns, and is equally effective applied as a finish, or as a surround to a panel of modelled leather.

STENCILLING. Stencilled leather decoration is simply a direct application of various types of colour to a surface of leather. Tea cosies, cushions, albums and articles of personal wear all lend themselves to this style. The stencil itself must be cut on stencil paper, which, being waterproof, fully safeguards the leather. The best results are obtained by spraying, as with this method various

LEATHERCRAFT

colours may be superimposed on each other, with unusual but pleasing contrasts. On light-coloured calf the result is easily obtained with the ordinary spirit stains, and on velvet Persian barbola colours or oils may be used. Be extremely careful in the colour application, especially upon small articles. Coloured inks applied to stencilled leather give quite reliable results in strong, bright colours. They are also easy to apply without danger of diffusing over the surrounding surface. Small dots and continuous lines may be applied with the ink. Be careful in using the brush not to flood on the colour; merely apply the colour from the point of the stencil-brush—and sparingly. On a large surface of stencilling, newspapers may be cut to cover the part of the leather to be "stopped" out when the spray is in use.

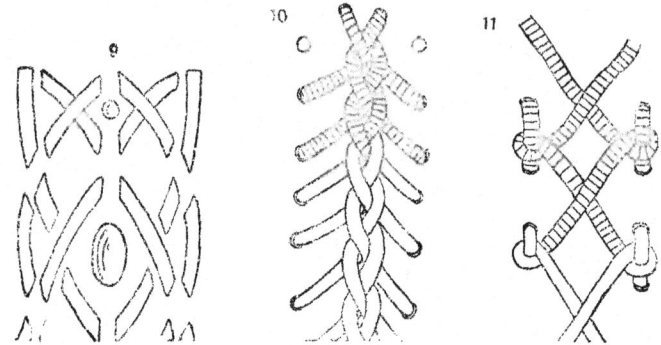

Process of thonging. 9. *Interlacing on flat surface, and combined with modelling.* 10. *Thonged border with circular thonging holes.* 11. *Thonged border.*

EXAMPLE OF STENCILLED LEATHERWORK. It will be observed in the cutting of a stencil that the design must "float" on the surface, which permits the surround of the stencil paper to be an entire flat plane. Otherwise, the colour would flood the underlying surface of leather.

THONGING—ITS DECORATIVE VALUE
PLAITING AND LACING

THONGED decorations in leatherwork are always satisfying; they seem to fulfil the natural demands of the material both in line and in section, and, as combined constructional and decorative agents, they are unrivalled. Thongs may be cut to all sizes, obtained in varied colourings, and may be procured from various skins. They are the recognised medium for the lacing and binding of bags, blotters, note-cases, purses and many other examples of leatherwork. Needlework with its wonderful variety of stitches and methods of securing fabrics together has something quite in common with the use of the thong in leatherwork.

A piece of well-thonged leather, entirely plain otherwise, is always a complete piece of craftsmanship. Therefore scrupulous care must be exercised in marking off the thonging holes to make certain of a perfect result when the thongs are introduced, for there is nothing in leatherwork that looks worse than badly spaced and applied thongs. Thonging is an excellent discipline for one's creative faculty, because here there is a large opportunity for experimenting in unusual and new methods. For example, broad and narrow thongs may be allied in one or several combinations, while contrasting colours and different skins will suggest innumerable possibilities to the alert worker. Calfskin thongs of the best quality are the most suitable thonging agent, with the skin of the

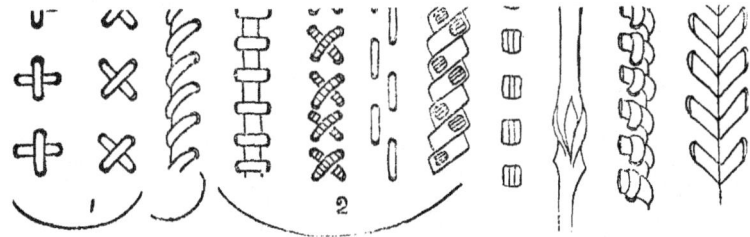

12. *Process of thonging.* 1. *As a binding (cross and herring-bone).* 2. *Interlacing on flat surface and combined with modelling.* 3. *Use of different colours in overcasting and formation of designs.*

Persian goat a good second. The clean, firm nature of the calfskin makes the thongs ideal for all first-class work. They can also be relied upon to harmonise well with other and varied leathers.

PREPARATION : THONGING. This is the next operation after the completion of the tooling, modelling and backing of the decoration. If it is a bag, pockets or inner fittings should be bound and assembled by machine stitching, unless they are made of light skiver. In that case turn the upper edges over to form a narrow lay and secure them with any reliable fixative, such as durofix, safegrip, or even a well-made flour paste. Arrange together all the edges of the bag, outside cover and inner pockets, and, if they are likely to be thick and cumbersome, pare the edges carefully to a uniform thickness. The blade of a safety razor mounted in wood makes an excellent paring knife. Now assemble the entire bag, using small brass paper-clips, which will hold the separate parts during the process of thonging. (*Fig.* 7.) It is not always practicable to fix the edges together with the fixative before thonging, but whenever it is possible, do so. With reference to the use of a gusset, refer to the description of small sundries in leather where their production and application are clearly explained (*p. 505*).

LEATHERCRAFT

13. Interlacing on flat surface.

In a general way it is not advisable to make the holes too far apart; an eighth of an inch is quite enough for the majority of articles, at a similar distance from the edge. But there can be no hard and fast rule, as each piece of work has its own individual problem. Sometimes a thong is overcast above another of different colour, which entirely alters the section and spacing.

The thong, before staining, is inclined to be too soft and pliable but it improves greatly after immersion into the liquid, and when dry it becomes firm and more agreeable to handle. Always polish a thong before inserting it into the leather. Thonging may be obtained in continuous lengths, but short thongs are preferable, as they are generally cut from a better part of the skin. To join two thongs, pare the surfaces with a safety razor blade, paring the underside of one thong and the top of the other to about 1 inch from the end of each, then a touch of durofix and a press with the fingers will fix them securely together. Allow them to remain under a moderate pressure for four or five minutes, when they will be ready for use. In the application of a thonged edging to any piece of leatherwork, always begin and end with the thongings in a position where they will be well hidden. Loose ends must on no account be visible. Taper the thongs before inserting them into the thonging hole, and if they are slit holes, apply a small piece of thin sheet-metal to the end of the thong with durofix: the work will be much easier.

In all thonging, carefully avoid pulling the thongs too tightly, as this would result in a puckered surface. Pull them firmly, and occasionally, as the thonging proceeds, give them a light tap with a mallet on a clean surface. This process will bed them into the seam and improve their finish.

DIFFERENT TYPES OF THONGING. Good effects are also obtained by using thongs in the form of interlaced patterns on flat surfaces, such as panels, screens, bags or similar articles. They lend themselves to varied colour tones ; while the natural thickness of the thongs in section result is pleasing.

INTERLACED THONGING COMBINED WITH MODELLING. They may also be used along with modelling, as in a Celtic decoration. For example, the head and wings of a bird could terminate in an elaborate interlacing of thonging. As the Celtic style is mainly composed of interlacing and plaited bosses of flat uniform strands, the natural line and section of a leather thong provides the requisite medium for such a decoration, for many colours and different weights of thong may be used, and the general scope of this style of leatherwork is unlimited. Extremely broad thonging is very effective on music stools, screens and other large pieces of leatherwork.

Colour schemes of infinite variety are possible with gold, silver and bronze thongs. Applied singly or in pairs they readily suggest a wide range of patterns. Blue combined with gold, green with silver, or bronze with a nut-brown leather are but a few examples. They may be designed as running borders, or as an overcasting, with one colour over or under the other. Applied in large or small squares to form a dice pattern, they will look pleasingly effective. The above are but a few groupings of colour and design which easily can be extended by the keen and progressive worker.

LEATHER APPLIQUÉ

APPLIQUÉ decoration in leather is practically the laying of one leather over the other in the natural or in many varied colour schemes. First-class work requires extreme care in the use of the punch, chisel, knife or scissors. It has a wide range of decorative possibilities where brilliant colours are introduced. It may also be applied in combination with modelled leather, and may be treated with tooled lines of varying weight to emphasise the

14. Example of leather appliqué.

pattern. The decoration introduced should be modern in character and without unnecessary detail, which is entirely unsuited for this style. Geometric units of squares, circles and triangles will provide suitable material for the grouping of conventional forms. Appliqué patterns may be carried out on the flat or in an embossed form. Flowers and fairly large details are best suited for this method. The parts in relief should have a light padding of cotton wool underneath, all the pieces being finally fixed to the ground with silk stitching : flat appliqué is applied with half thongs.

When transferring the design to the leather for appliqué, draw it first on thin paper, then apply it to the reverse side of the velvet Persian with flour paste and allow it to dry thoroughly, when it may be cut through the paper and leather easily and quickly. Afterwards remove the design and paste from the skin with a wet sponge. As a general rule all light skins cut easier through a layer of thin paper. Details requiring application of the knife will cut more freely with a sheet of glass underneath the leather.

When thonging appliqué to a body of leather, do so with velvet Persian, as it will give soft and finished edges. Join up the thongs by cutting one end to half its original width, then thread it through two or three holes, securing it into position with durofix. Now cut the end off flush with the edge of the work, and with a new thong commence on the inside of the leather three holes back, covering the narrow tapering end of the old thong previously inserted. Finally fix it in position with the fixitive for a few minutes, when the joining may be completed with the new thong. Appliqué decoration is suited for cushions, nightdress-cases and similar articles.

Mosaic, Inlay, Overlay and Patchwork in Leather

A MOSAIC or inlay decoration in leather might be compared to a form of jig-saw pattern, where varied shapes and colours are pieced together. The method depends almost entirely upon the accurate cutting and harmonious spacing of the material. To cut the leather accurately, have it resting on a sheet of glass, tile or strawcard. The scissors may also be utilised on velvet Persians, and cutting will be easier if the leather is first applied to a sheet of thin smooth paper. Almost any type of leather may be used in this work, although the velvet Persians, with their variety of colours, offer a wide appeal. Carver's chisels are extremely useful as cutting agents. The use of either straight or curved forms makes possible a clean, perfect incision by a direct hand-pressure of the tool. Some of the edges of the leather may require paring ; do this with the hot blade of a small knife, and you will be sure of a perfect assembling of the different pieces.

Conventional designs are most suitable for this style—planned mainly in a lay-out of harmonious spacing and dainty colour schemes. In cutting the mosaic to receive the inlay of leather, aim at clean-cut edges with their equivalent parts for insertion all perfect fits. The units of design may be fixed with Durofix or Seccotine, applied with scrupulous care. When perfectly " caught " and in position, apply a reasonable pressure to the surface of the inlaid leather, placing a layer of blotting paper between the weight and the inlay to keep it clean. Mosaic leather may be arranged in narrow, surrounding bands to divide the different sections and colours of a design. It may also be applied with the edges of the inlaid pieces in close contact with one another.

OVERLAY DECORATION. This embraces units of leather of various weights, shapes and colours applied to a surface in sections. It is the line and nature of the section which determine its success. A flat area such as a box lid may have units of leather introduced on

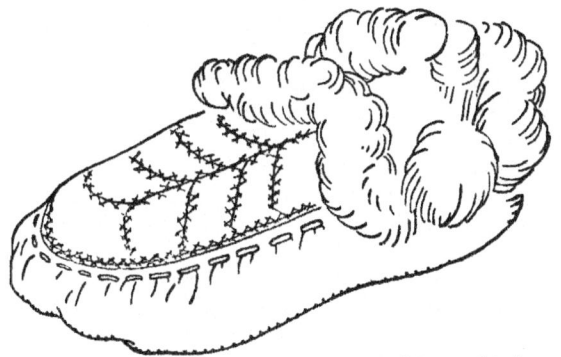

15. *Moccasin—leather patchwork (applied by stitching).*

its surface in superimposed layers with a very unusual decorative effect. For example, a square of dark-brown leather may form the base, a square of blue, slightly smaller in size, may then be placed over it, this followed by another square of brown still smaller, and the whole secured on the top by a knot made from a gold thong. Different shapes of leather, weights, and colour schemes may be repeated in this way and superimposed on one another with equal success.

Overlays in leather afford scope for original ideas in decoration. Where section and unique elevation are desired, the above style is most adaptable. Plaited borders or applied interlacings may also be introduced as sectional additions to another surface of leather.

PATCHWORK IN LEATHER. This is based on the same idea as mosaic, but it is neither so intricate in make-up nor so fine in quality. The patchwork pieces may be cut from odd scraps to any desired shapes and colour scheme, and may be used for moccasins, vanity bags, nightdress-cases and innumerable other articles. The patches may be secured with a fixitive to an underlying surface of leather or assembled and sewn together by hand or by machine.

BINDING. Thongs are generally employed for the binding of patchwork leather and, with a suitable colour scheme, gold, silver or bronze thonging is extremely effective in this work. Cross or herring-bone thonging ensure the most reliable and decorative finish.

In any of the aforementioned styles of decoration it is advisable to cut out the shapes required in thick paper first of all ; then place or fix the patterns on the reverse side of the leather and cut round them.

CARVED LEATHERWORK

GOOD results are obtainable in this style, but the leather must be stained to a dark tone to provide the necessary contrast for the carving. The incised tooling looks most effective on dead black. For leather carving the smallest veiner and one or two small straight and half-round gouges will be necessary. To ensure success sharp, clean-cutting chisels are absolutely essential, along with some initial practice. The veiner (carving tool) will be the principal implement in the work. The leather must be smooth, heavy calf or cowhide. If too thin the tool is liable to pierce the skin. Apply the tool in a horizontal position, and aim at a shallow cut just sufficient to produce a narrow, uniform groove or hollow on the leather surface. Against the darker tone the natural tone of the skin will appear. In cutting the groove on the leather, stop the incisions where the pattern interlaces ; this will give the effect of the one line passing over and under the other alternately. Cut the incisions on perfectly dry leather ; if damp, the leather is liable to pull, and this is unsatisfactory.

INCISED LEATHER

INCISED or cut leather is a more ambitious method of leather decoration. It has a distinct similarity to modelled leather, only it is a more perfect treatment. The actual tooling is generally of a finer quality, and the outline is cut with the incising knife. Great care and skill must be exercised in the use of the knife, as a too severe pressure of the blade will result in a slitting of the skin. This must be carefully avoided. The entire outline of a design may be cut only at certain well-chosen parts where strong shadows or bold relief occur. Cut the incisions with the leather resting on sheet-glass, firm strawboard, or a surface of wood. Cut on the dry leather, as in this condition it keeps cleaner, and with the blade in good condition can be easily worked. The knife may also be

LEATHERCRAFT

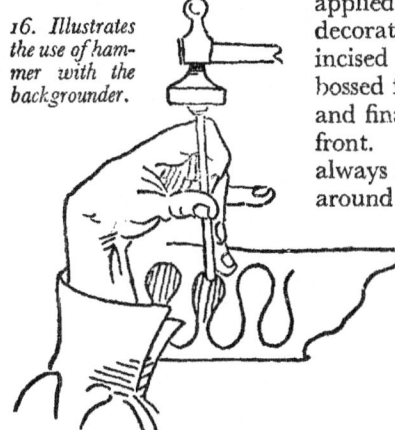

16. *Illustrates the use of hammer with the backgrounder.*

applied to the damp leather. Cut leather decoration may be treated as a flat incised outline only, or it may be embossed from the obverse side, reversed, and finally finished by modelling on the front. When work is being modelled, always introduce a soft, shallow hollow around the entire outline of the design, and slightly within the cut of the knife. The incisions made with the knife must now be opened with the tracer, using the sharp or blunt tool to suit either deep or light incisions. The freeing of the cut edges will result in a delicate tool line appearing around the entire outline of the design. It is this soft, delicate shadow which gives incised leather its attractiveness. The repoussé punches as applied in metalwork may be used with good results on incised or modelled leather, e.g. where some part of the design requires emphasis, or in providing a background for a decoration.

Backgrounds in leather are most effective when executed with the hammer and punch. They are easy to apply and the result is always satisfying as they ensure uniform depth and pleasing surface texture. The square-faced backgrounder will prove quite a useful

17. *Example of incised leather with background and press studs combined with the decoration.*

tool for the work. Various other forms of ground are possible with the use of mats and pearl punches. However, a plain, tooled surface is usually more effective.

With the completion of the background and the leather perfectly dry the work may be polished.

Metallic Thonging Lamellé

LAMELLÉ is a narrow, thin band of metal applied to the leather in addition to, or as a substitute for, the leather thong. It may be obtained in any metal and rolled to suit the purchaser's requirements of weight and breadth, which will save cutting by the worker. Do not overdo the polishing of the completed article after inserting

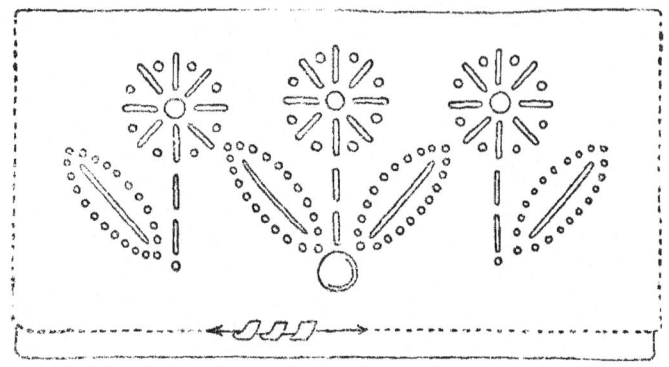

18. Metallic lamellé—combined with punched stencil decoration.

lamellé, as the skin of lacquer, applied to preserve the burnished surface of the metal, may be broken and oxidation would follow. Mark off the holes for the metallic thonging with spring dividers and slit them with a small straight chisel to suit the breadth of the thongs. Metallic thonging may be used in innumerable ways with striking effect, according to the colour scheme and the purpose of the article. This type of thonging produces an effect similar to that of gold and silver thonging in leather, only the metal bands are firmer and, applied constructionally, add to the strength of the work. The thongs in metal look particularly well if arranged in dice pattern, in strapwork, or in continuous borders. They also furnish fresh and pleasing suggestions for a combined grouping of leather with other materials.

Metal and Leather Combined

METAL and leather form a pleasing combination in many articles of leatherware, so an intelligent knowledge of metalwork is a decided acquisition to the leatherworker. Bag frames, hinges, piercings and panels in repoussé metal all find their use in the production of leatherware, while, for ornamental purposes, gold and silver as well as the baser metals may be introduced. Well-designed letters can even be purchased ready for mounting to the leather, many delightful clasps and other fittings easily applied, and unique and pleasing effects derived by removing the celluloid facing from the press studs which lock the bags. The original surfaces of these can be replaced by tooled metal studs finished with gold or silver on very special work. This device gives a much less ordinary effect and increases the value of the article. Metal fasteners other than the press stud may also be introduced with interesting results.

Another and charming method of combining constructional and decorative materials may be employed by studding small boxes, etc., with little brass-headed nails. This style of decoration is merely a revival of an old-time village craft practised by the shoemakers and saddlers. Leather covered trunks of all sizes were bound and decorated with leather in a delightful pattern of brass-headed nails. Nails for purposes such as this may be obtained in convenient sizes in almost any section, shape and colour of metal. " Cloutage " is the term applied to their use in leatherwork. Not only do they provide unusual opportunity for artistic designing but they also greatly simplify the application of leather to a surface of wood.

Staining, Marbling and Spraying

LEATHER may be purchased in a natural tone or in a wide variety of colours. It may also be treated with surface tinting, for, though the quiet tone of the natural leather has much to commend it, it is easily soiled, and so is not quite so suitable for some articles. The value and use of stains, inks, paint and other colour mediums, therefore, are worthy of consideration. Stains may be obtained already prepared in liquid form, or as a powder. If bought in the latter form, the stain is prepared by mixing the powder with methylated spirit, preferably in a long, narrow bottle, which will suit the long tube of the spray.

SPRAYING. This is a most effective method of applying colour. It is simple and lends itself to numerous treatments. Careful spraying in the usual way results in a uniform and perfectly even tone, but the stain may also be vapourised to the leather as a mere mist of colour. Again, colour may be applied with the small brush or small pads of cotton wool so that the stains are worked skilfully through each other. The pen, or a very fine brush is most suitable for the application of the coloured inks, particularly where fine lines or small details of bright colour are desired.

MARBLING AND SPRINKLING. On leather this is a type of

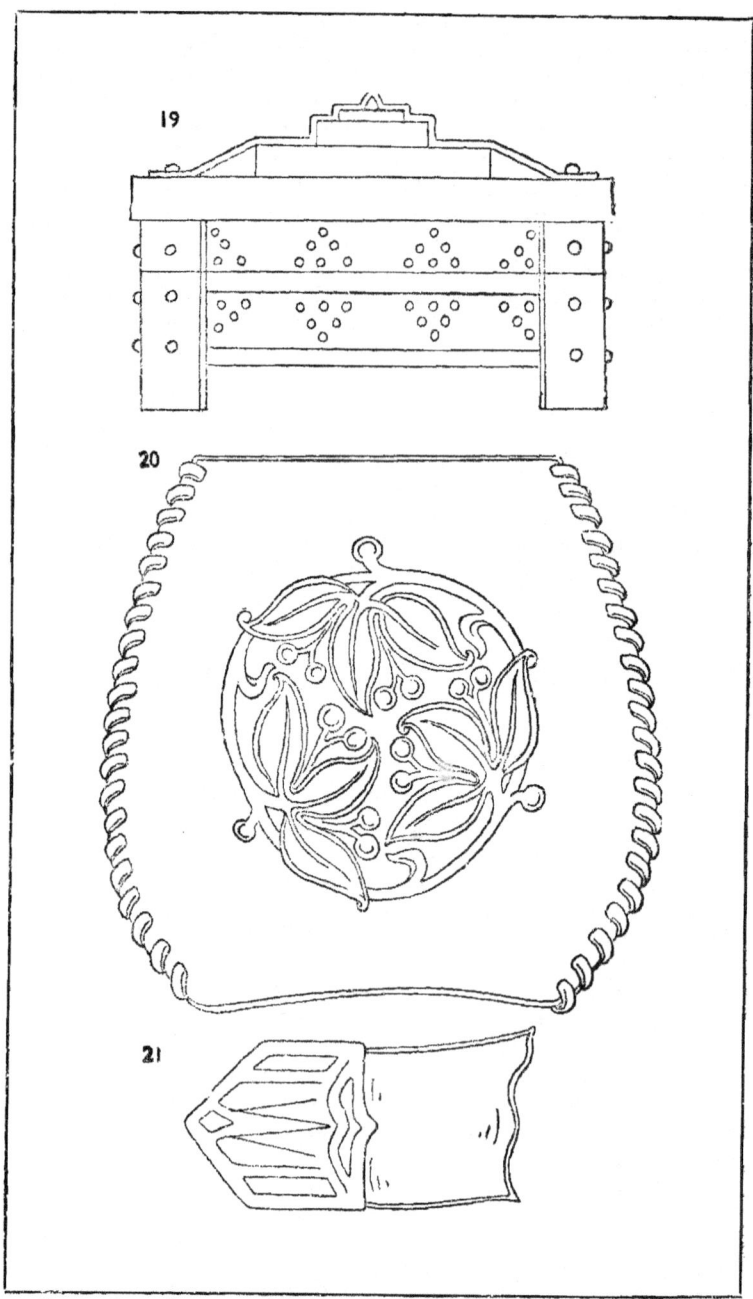

19. Box—colour scheme emerald green calf with pewter fittings. 20. Bag in repoussé silver. 21. Terminal of belt—pierced silver.

decoration that can be made extremely effective. The process of sprinkling simply lies in passing small drops of colour in varying shades on to the leather according to plan. Tree-marbling on leather, too, affords plenty of scope for experimental and original work. Irregular patterns may be cut out in paper and the surround left pasted to a leather surface on the same principle as stencil work. The open spaces should then be sprinkled with drops of rich colour, and only when these are quite dry may the paper be removed. The effect of colour applied in this way is really striking.

Scorching and Tinting with the Platinum Point

This form of decoration can be effectively combined with other mediums and styles. A rich tone of sepia may be attained by a careful and moderate use of the pokerwork tool. Every precaution must be exercised in its use, however, as leather is easily ruined with excessive heat. A deft control of the platinum point is essential to good work, and demands a high standard of artistic ability. The hot tool may be applied to any leather, ordinary calf, cowhide, pigskin and basil being most suitable for the purpose. Apply the platinum with light delicate touches, and endeavour to capture the varying shades of brown which harmonise with the natural tone of the leather. Colour may be introduced along with the scorching, but generally the latter is more effective alone.

Batik on Leather

Batik as a decorative agent on leather is rather unusual as it is more commonly associated with textiles. It depends upon a slightly scorched effect produced by covering certain parts of the surface of the leather with hot wax. The degree of heat required on a surface of calf is just sufficient to give that shade of light, rich brown which blends perfectly with the fawn of the natural skin. Calfskin, cowhide and a fine basil are the most suitable surfaces for batik—but calf for preference. A strong, broad jazz pattern will give the best result.

Melt some candle-wax and with it fill in the design, using a brush in slick, direct strokes and allowing an irregular spot at random to give additional interest and effect. A special tool which retains the molten wax may be obtained, but, with a little practice, the brush will prove quite as good. When the wax is set, immerse the entire surface under cold, running water; this will effectively release the wax from the leather, when the pleasing tone of the scorching will be readily apparent. The exposed parts of the pattern on the leather may now be enriched with the coloured inks. Another variation may be obtained by spraying the surround of the natural leather before removing the wax. Any wax which is difficult to remove will cake off if the leather is bent to right and left when under the running tap. Successful results in this style of work depend mainly upon the possession of a certain " flair " for novelty and a good sense of colour.

Cuir Bouilli

MODELLING in cuir bouilli is a specially prepared leather subjected to hand-moulding. Cuttings of leather may be used up in this way, and must first be thoroughly soaked in a jar of water. The continued immersion reduces the leather to a plastic condition like that of modelling clay or wax, so that in this form it will respond freely to the pressure of the fingers. For the production of buttons, mouldings and original sections on coffers, small figures and objects of a similar nature, it will be found very suitable.

Engraved Leather

ENGRAVED leather results from application of the tool just as in woodcarving, only the work is much finer and suitable for small detail. The incised line may be cut on light-toned or on dark leather. Its result depends mainly on a rich, delicate treatment, combined with strong colour. Use the coloured inks in the work. The graver is applied in a thin incision of one breadth, and this section is then treated with colour applied from the point of a fine pen. Another effective result may be obtained by slightly spraying the entire surface after engraving the line. Thongs may also be enhanced by the addition of the smart, narrow line of the graver applied directly in the centre of the thong. Cross-cut patterns may also be introduced as a novelty in application. The general effect of this decoration is Florentine in character. As a decoration it is only suitable for light articles, such as cigarette-cases, pocket-books, diaries and similar work.

Flowers, Tassels, Chains, Buttons, and Small Sundries in Leather

FLOWERS in suéde leather afford a wide scope for new ideas to an imaginative worker. In making these avoid hackneyed imitations of nature, and strive rather for a conventional and decorative treatment. Cut the shapes of the petals and leaves in stiff paper, fold them into divisions of four, six or eight, and then cut the leather to the same shape with small sharp scissors. Innumerable patterns and petal-shapes will suggest themselves. Insert a spot or " eye " of brilliant colour to provide a sparkle. Tiny circles of gold, silver or felt cut with a punch may be introduced with telling effect. Powdered gold or silver may also be applied in like fashion.

The possibilities of floral treatment are unlimited to the keen and ingenious worker. They may be applied as a flat decoration, or as appliqués gummed or stitched to cushions, slippers, waistcoats and other articles of personal wear.

Tassels in leather are frequently used as finishings on cushions and handles of bags, and as decorations on kilt sporrans in Highland dress. They are made mainly by cutting or slashing to a fringe with the scissors circles of leather of varied diameter and weight. They are then fixed at the centre, drawn down from it and secured in the form of a tassel.

Suéde leather will prove best for tassels on cushions and light work generally : calf for the better and stronger type. These are developed mainly from single and compound plaits grouped together in circles and thonged tightly towards the top. They are more easy to make if wrought over a wooden mould, or developer, from a knot of leather strands.

Chains and buttons are also important sundries in leatherware. Such articles as waist-belts, bag handles, and all work of a similar nature originate from them. Marginal edgings of leather may all be applied in a decorative form. When the skin is cut with the knife or shears it is liable to appear crude and lacking finish. This may be rectified by scalloping the edge or using some similar device on the leather. Small outlines of perforated holes are also extremely well suited to edge decoration.